Real Estate Investing

The Ultimate Guide to Making Income on Housing Properties

By

Stephen Baker

INTRODUCTION

Thank you for downloading this book!

Do you want your money to work for you even when you are sleeping? Are you unsure about how to invest your money wisely? Or are you simply curious about the how investing in real estates can bring wealth? Well, you are not alone!

Since the beginning of civilization, those who own plots of land have often been associated with power, wealth and placed in high regards in the society. This is from whence the term "land-LORD" was created. Lord of the land – influential and rich. It is of no coincidence that even today, owning lands and developing properties still continue to bring in vast amounts of wealth for selected individuals. Donald Trump, Li Ka Shing – just to name a few.

Because of its association with money, many people wonder if real estate investing is a game only for the rich and that without an enormous amount of starting capital, there is simply no way to jump into it.

Well, the answer is absolutely not! There is no rule cast in stone that says you need to a millionaire to benefit from it.

In fact, this very book will guide you on the fundamental concepts of real estate investing and provide you with clear, actionable steps on how to make a decent income from real estate investment from scratch.

You will also understand tips and tricks of the trade that allow you make astute investment decisions in order to get the most "bang" for your bucks. After all, who doesn't like a good bargain?

Yes, all forms of investments carry a certain amount of risk but they are definitely not rocket science. As long as you understand the risks involved as well as the things you can do to mitigate them, you will be duly rewarded in time.

Smart investing doesn't have to be complicated. If you are keen to find out more, then let us dive straight into this exciting journey of real estate investing. Read on to find out more!

Once again, thank you for downloading this book and taking your brave first step into the world of real estates.

Table of Contents

CHAPTER 1.

WHAT IS REAL ESTATE INVESTING?

What exactly qualifies as a real estate investment? In fact, what does investing in real estate even mean? Before we get into the mechanics of this form of investment vehicle, we need to first understand its fundamentals.

Now, there are literally hundreds of ways to make money in real estate. Certain methods require more time invested than others but the truth is - the amount of time you spent in this business largely boils down to your strategy, your ability to read the markets, your knowledge and your own personality.

In a nutshell, a real estate investment is akin to buying a piece of property, which is not a primary residence, with the aim of using it to generate income over time. It is not uncommon for investors to own multiple pieces of real estate and using them to generate income through collecting rental and profits through price appreciation.

Some common examples of investment properties are apartment buildings and rental houses, in which the owners do not live in the residential units, but use them to generate rental income from tenants.

It is also a very common misconception that your house (a residential property) is an investment. Yes, your house may undergo appreciation in value over the years but appreciation does not decide if a property is a good investment! In fact, personal residential property makes really bad investment. It costs money every month to maintain, requires constant attention, and will probably never appreciate in value more than the amount it costs you to hold each month. Let us assume that you are putting down about $1,500 per month on a mortgage payment and about $100 on maintenance and repair. You are, in fact, losing $19,200 annually! It is very difficult to find a house that appreciates $19,200 a year. Another way of looking at it is that if you purchase a property and you rent it out completely, you receive income. However, if you live in it, the property takes away income from you because of maintenance fees and miscellaneous upkeep. A property that takes money away from you month after month is hardly an investment at all.

On the other hand, a property that you purchased and rent out completely will generate a consistent flow of cash flow for you. This, then, becomes a real asset or an investment.

With that said, an excellent real estate investor has to invest for both price appreciation and generating cash flow and not forsake one for the other. The key is to carefully evaluate the property and doing research pre-purchase, as well as making sure that you source for the best tenants in the post-purchase phase.

Do you have to be a "guru" to be successful in real estate investing? Absolutely not! There are countless investors that have become very successful in this field without the help of gurus. In fact, many people from this crowd aim to sell you on the dream of fast riches, easy money and luxurious lifestyle. They prey on the people who desperately want to make money and often use slick salesmanship to get you to buy very expensive courses and training. The reason why I'm telling you this is because there is no reason for real estate investing to be complicated at all, and I believe that everybody should be given a chance to start on a level playing field. Why should you start the journey losing a few thousand dollars upfront?

By now you should have realized that owning a piece of real estate is quite an attractive proposition! Who doesn't like an extra $2000 to $4000 dollars of passive income every month? To many, this is almost the equivalence of their monthly paycheck. You must also be wondering if real estate investment is the best way to make your money work for you. After all, everybody likes to pick the road with the least resistance, right? In the next chapter, we are going to see how investing in property fares against other forms of passive income strategies.

CHAPTER 2.

REAL ESTATE VS OTHER INCOME STREAMS

Passive income is, according to many people, the holy grail of making money. It is the art of making money even when you are in a passive state and not working at all. Now, there are many ways to create passive income streams, and different people traverse different routes to meet at the top. Why should you choose to invest in real estate? Why not the stock market or create a business and sell some products?

Well, the first thing that you need to understand when it comes to working for passive income is that you need to be doing this for a reason other than money. If you have a day job and you hate it, you are only going to make your life more miserable by finding a side job that you equally dislike. Why pile on the misery? Ultimately, that means that you need to be doing this because you're truly interested about what it is you're deciding to supplement your income with.

If you have absolutely no interest in real estate or dislike the hassle of managing tenants, there are probably far better ways for you to invest your money. But if have downloaded this book, I'm convinced that you are driven enough to start on this journey.

What then makes real estate investing stand out from the herd?

First of all, real estate investing provides cash flow. And by cash flow, we are talking about significant amounts. It is not uncommon to receive passive cash flow of $1000 to $4000 a month on a $50,000-$100,000 investment! This is almost as good as investing in a dividend paying stock that pays 1%-8% dividend every month.

Real estate on the whole has also seen an appreciation in price that trumps over other forms of financial investment vehicles. Let's look at a recent 13-year comparison of real estate and stock market, from 2000-2013, during the worst housing crash of our lifetime.

The average sales price for a single-family residence at the beginning of 2000 was $138,000 according to the National Association of Realtors. By 2013, the average sales price for a single-family residence had risen to $216,600. Despite the housing crash, the value of the initial investment added $78,600 in value – a 57% increase. This means $100,000 invested in real estate in 2000 would have been worth $157,000 thirteen years later. This is a very decent $366 increase in value every month even without factoring rental income.

Another good reason to invest in real estate is because of leverage. We will go through this concept in detail in a later chapter, essentially, you are able to invest in a $100,000 property with only $30,000 in cash! By being able to put less money down on a home than the actual cost, the advantages of rental properties are multiplied. Of course, it is also possible to leverage money with stocks by buying on a margin. But stock margins can be called if the stock decrease in value. Additionally, you can never hold a stock on margin for as long as you can on a piece of property!

Many people feel that the best way to make passive income is by starting a business or starting some sort of affiliate marketing business. Sure, if the business takes off, the reward can be immense! But let's face it, not everybody makes the cut to do business. You need to figure out what is audience want, you need to know how to make a great product, you need to have the right distribution channel, you have sell and market the product and to top it off, you need a significant slice of luck to be successful. Now, I'm not discouraging you to pursue this path, but if your goal is to settle on a stable source of passive income, there are definitely easier ways to get there! As opposed to starting a business that is full of uncertainties, real estate investing is much more understandable and predictable. Each investment follows a similar set of checklist to go through, which is the main reason why investing in properties is beginner-friendly.

CHAPTER 3.

BE EDUCATED

If you want to be the best in this field, you need to understand the lingo of the game. This chapter might seem a little boring but it is an essential chapter to study in order to get yourself up to speed. Here are some basic terminologies you have be familiar with:

1) Income:

Income is simply the amount of money that you make from an investment source. This math is perhaps the easiest of all: simply add up the amount of rent and any additional fees that comes in.

For example – you own a property. The home rents for $1000, and the tenant also pays $25 for the use of the garage. The total income will be $1,025.

2) Expense:

Expenses are the things that cost you money in an investment. For example, household maintenance for an apartment is $100 per month, the bank loan costs $400 a month and the utilities are $50 a month. The total of these expenses will be $550.00.

3) Cash Flow:

Cash flow is simply the amount of money left over at the end of the month after all expenses are paid. We have mentioned previously that in order to qualify a property as a good investment, it should provide you with cash flow month over month.

4) Return on Investment:

Your "return on investment" (also known as ROI) is a term used to describe the percentage of your money you make on your initial investment in a year. For example, if you invested $300 and you made $150 from that investment over the course of one year, you would have made a 50% return on investment.

A simple example for using ROI to calculate an investment return would be: On a certain date, you put $2000 into your bank account. Exactly 1 year from the date you put this amount in, you will have $2200 in that same account. Your ROI on the investment is:

Total ROI = (2200 − 2000) / (2000) = 10%

This simple mathematics present the foundations upon which almost all other real estate calculations are based.

In fact, in every investment, the term ROI is freely used to describe the potential return. Obviously, the higher the potential ROI or actual ROI, the better the investment is. Most of the time, if an investment is projected to have high ROI, it will be priced at a premium rate, making the initial cost of investment higher as well.

5) Wholesaling:

Whole sailing is an advanced terminology that you need to be exposed to. A wholesaler, in a nutshell, puts property (normally distressed property) under contract and assigns or resells the property to another investor. The investors or the buyer either use cash, lines of credit, or hard money loans. This allows quick closings on properties that sometimes need extensive repairs. A wholesaler is a proponent of the idea of "money solves all issues". He believes that if you can sell a property for a low enough price, somebody will eventually buy it, regardless if there are any problems with the property. A wholesaler has two main job scopes – finding suitable deals to close and expanding their network of investors to sell to. Wholesaling real estate provides an opportunity for someone to build income with little capital or credit.

6) Property Types:

The following list includes the most common property types that you are likely to deal with as a real estate investor. Although you don't have to deal with all of them, it is always wise to know them in case you want to niche down:

- Raw Land: Raw land is nothing but a piece of earth or grass patch. This land can be improved, leased or rented to create cash flow. Most raw lands are sold to investors or property developers who want to construct properties on the land to generate higher revenues.

- Single Family Home: Single family homes are very common and it is very easy to rent, sell or finance. This is also the reason why SFHs are very popular among new investors and home flippers alike. However, choosing a location is important for SFH investors because in many places, the rental generates from SFHs are quite low to be a substantial amount.

- Duplex/Triplex: Small multifamily properties are probably one of the best real estate investments out there. They are easy to finance and easy to sell or rent. They also generate a much higher amount of cash flow than SFHs. Many times, an investor would buy a Triplex and take up residence in one of the units, this allows him to better manage the properties. When securing loan from the bank, you only need to get a single loan to purchase the multiple units, which is an advantage over trying to secure a loan per unit when you buy other properties.

- REIT: Real Estate Investment Trust is essentially a mutual fund for real estate. Many people come to together and invest in this fund in order to purchase large real estate investments usually worth multiple millions of dollars. Profits from this investments are then distributed among the investors. Investing in REITs is usually a very hands off approach and but the returns from this approach also align more with buying a stock or fund. Dividend from REITs is, however, relatively higher.

Of course, this list is non-exhaustive and to truly understand the topic of real estate is an entire university degree's worth of workload on its own. We have barely scratched the surface. However, the goal is to equip you with the essential knowledge and develop your confidence so that you are able to navigate this industry on your own. One of the key things that hinders a person from starting out is the fear of stepping out of his comfort zone; he is scared that the investment he put will never come back; he is afraid that once he bought a property, there will be a repeat of 2008.

There are too many people who know that they should make a positive change in their lives, but yet, they do not materialize that positive thinking into quantifiable results. They sit on their hands thinking that perhaps one day, they can overcome their habit of hesitation just by thinking about it. Life can become a movie sometimes when we are the ones sitting back and watch it pass us by. We make so many commitments to make our lives better but we always seem to be stuck in the inertia phase. Simply put, if you don't take action, you will regret it. Here is a list of actionable steps, which will help you get on your feet and start those engines:

1) Have A Plan

If you are looking to real estate investing to save you from a job you hate, then you had better start working to replace the income from your job with money made from real estate activities. Plan a schedule for yourself so that you will not sit on your hands and think about what to do every day. Know what you what to achieve within a certain time frame. Do not expect to purchase one property and live off it forever – truly successful people are always working hard to improve themselves!

2) Stay Committed

Yes, learning from gurus may help you gain more knowledge, but there has to be a time where you stop watching those videos or reading these books. Stop spending unnecessary money until you manage to stay committed to the cause. The real secret to successful investing lies in what goes on in between your ears. Realize that you could spend a lot of money having someone show the mechanics, but if you are not willing to deal with the "conditioning" issue, you are just wasting money.

3) Start Participating

This is fairly straightforward but often difficult to achieve. Get out there and expose yourself to the community and learn the ropes by applying your concepts! Don't just hang around online forums procrastinating; participate, ask questions, connect with others, and build relationships. If you are afraid to ask questions, then you are going to be just as afraid to speak with a seller who needs to sell you their property or to negotiate with a big city developer. Interactions are part of an investor's life, so the faster you can overcome this fear, the more successful you'll be.

4) Mastering Basics

Without knowing the lingo of a real estate investor, you will always be afraid of sounding like you don't know what you are talking about. Once you build up your confidence in understanding the language of real estate investors, you will have the confidence and ability to communicate with your partners.

Once you have mastered the previous step, you need to start understanding the concepts. If you can't adequately explain what debt-to-income is or why 70% ARV is important in a house flip, you need to spend more time learning. Fear is often a result of being unclear. Additionally, once you have a good understanding, you give back to the system by teach someone else in your network. In fact, teaching someone else a concept will help to cement your own understanding of the topic into your mind.

All investment has some degree of risk, and real estate investing is no exception. While risk can't be avoided, it can be managed through proper preparation, which you have already begun by reading this guide. The hardest thing to do in any new venture is to get started, at some point, you have to tell yourself to just get down to it!

CHAPTER 4.

FAST MONEY: FLIPPING PROPERTIES

If you have watched real estate investment TV shows, you will find that there are people who are consistently able to buy an ugly house, fix it up in a few weeks and then selling it for insane amount of profit. Well, if something looks too good to be true, it probably is! The truth is – house flipping is a lot harder than it looks. It takes hard work, education and a lot of experience to flip houses. But it is definitely possible and even a lot of fun. Just to give you an idea, I've known people who bought houses at $50,000 and flipping them a few weeks later for $100,000 - that's 100% ROI in slightly more than a month! Many people do not classify this way as investing because investing traditionally involves the act of "buy and hold". However, flipping CAN be an investment if you use it as a tool to generate income to support a more robust investment strategy. In other words, flipping can help either pay the bills (like a job) or used as a source of cash infusion into your investment strategy. However, don't assume you will simply "flip your way to retirement."

When fixing and flipping more expensive houses, you should make more money than the less expensive flips. The more expensive a house, the more interest, the more repairs, more holding costs and more commissions you pay. For the increased risk on a more expensive house, you should aim to be rewarded with more profits.

If you are looking for some key steps to fix-and-flip success, check out the list below!

1) *Research* – As with doing anything, you need to know what you are getting yourself into. You need to do exhaustive research on the location prior to buying the house and you need to understand the local housing market scene to understanding the purchasing power of your potential buyers.

2) *Networking* – To flip a house, you have to be constantly sniffing out good deals. Doing this on your own is incredibly hard work because of the huge amount of time you have to spend on doing research. A great way to shorten this process is by networking with local investors and realtors. Building a good relationship with these people will help immensely especially if they give you first dips on a potential good deal.

3) *Raising Capital* – Sometimes you might see a really good deal but are unable to cough up the cash to nail it. Therefore, it is a good idea to find investors who can actually finance your purchase. You can find them at REIA meetings, networking events and chambers of commerce.

If these fails, you can always try your luck with family, friends and business partners.

4) *Assemble a team* – Let's face it – you cannot fo everything yourself. Building a team is critical to your fix-and-flip success. As a beginner, you might need to consult lawyers, accountants and real estate agents. You will also have to find an efficient team of designers and workers to ensure that your house is renovated into the way you want it to be.

5) *Locate and analyze* – If you don't have the time to source for houses in great locations, you can always assign a real estate agent to do it for you. However, you must understand that real estate agents make money through buying and selling houses and this can lead to a conflict of interest. You should always let them have a clear idea of what you are after and let it be known to them to have your best interests in mind when sourcing for a deal. After a candidate house has been shortlisted, compare its value to the value of other properties so you can a rough idea of what you are getting yourself into.

6) Offering – Many people stumbled at this obstacle because it's when they part with their money. You have to overcome this fear and stay committed to the cause if you really want to make it in real estate.

7) Selling the property – After you are happy with the fix, it's time to make sure that you actually turn your effort into profits by selling the house. This is where your networking skills can pay off again. Tap on your network to seek out a suitable buyer to close the deal!

Hopefully this short guide has shown that it with hard work and due diligence, it is possible to flip houses and make profits. Before we end this chapter, I want to share 2 important precautionary tips with you before you dive into the world of house flipping.

- Be conservative in your calculations. This will ensure that you have a wide safety margin in case the investment does not pan out the way you want it to. For example, when calculating your costs, always assume that the eventual expense is going to be at least 30% higher than what you plan to fork out.

- Have a backup plan. What if nobody wants to buy your house? What if the value of your house plummets? These are real (as unlikely as they can be) scenarios that can happen to your strategy. Always have a backup plan so that you are prepared for it. For example, before you buy the house, make sure that in the event that you are unable to sell the house, you are still able to find suitable tenants for the property.

CHAPTER 5.

SOURCES OF CAPITAL

Raising funds to finance a real estate investment is often one of the biggest obstacle an investor can face. Most of the time, an investor need not pay the full sum of the transaction up front, but the earnest money deposit can still prove to be a stumbling roadblock to many.

What is an earnest money deposit? When you want to purchase a house as investment, you usually have to put up a sum of money upfront as earnest money. This is a sign of goodwill from the buyer. In some cases, instead of placing earnest deposits, sellers will want the buyer to place a 10%-20% down payment up front in order to close the deal. If you are currently living paycheck-to-paycheck, coughing up this amount of money (usually $10,000-$50,000) can be very difficult. However, fortunately, raising capital isn't rocket science. Here are a few excellent ways to raise the necessary money to fund your purchase:

1) Institutional Investors through a LLC - You can seek for professional investors if you set up a company. However, when you're dealing with other people's money, you need to make sure you are setup correctly. If you plan on raising money with an LLC, start by registering your LLC in the

state where you will be working out of. Many people make the mistake of not registering their LLC with the right state entity. If things go wrong for your investors, you will likely land in trouble. What you want to do is to draft an operating agreement that states how the fund will be used and managed. This is a crucial step for any investor because this agreement keeps everyone in the loop as to how the funds will be handled.

2) Friends and Family - Yes, you can receive funding from your loved ones. Banks and investors might not be willing to risk money on you but those who are close to you might be willing to give you the chance to have a shot in the dark. What you want to do is to draft up a business plan on how their money will be managed and what is the expected return on their investment, if any. Be frank and transparent about the risks involved. You should also encourage your loved ones to be as honest as possible and show you some tough love. It is always helpful to hear honest opinions from a few third parties on how they view this piece of investment.

3) Bank Loan - Going through banks, credit unions and other home mortgage companies is a great way right now to finance a real estate investment. Rates are currently at 6.25% for a 30-year fixed or 5.75% for a 15-year fixed rate. However, because of the subprime housing dilemma,

traditional lenders have tightened their lending criteria. Most require a 680 credit score or better for approval. Most institutions will ask for documentation of your income statement and debts in order to be qualified for the loan. If you qualify, the down payment is usually 10%, although this rate may vary. We highly recommend this method for beginners because it is the most traditional, safe and well-known way finance your investment.

4) Lease optioning - If you really cannot find the cash to fund your investment right now, you can do a lease option. Lease option allows an investor to own the property for little or no money. The idea is that you will eventually pay the money back, usually within the next 2-3 years. This gives you a grace period to source for sufficient financing to carry out the purchase.

5) FHA Loan - The Federal Housing Administration (FHA) is a United States government program that insures mortgages for banks. The idea behind this is that money is pooled to spread risk across the entire population. FHA loans are only permitted to people who are buying properties to live in but investors can take advantage of this rule to buy houses with multiple units and then subsequently renting out the empty units. FHA loans

typically only require a 3.5% down payment so you can get started much quicker.

CHAPTER 6.

HOW TO FIND PROPERTIES

Up until now, we have been talking about how to get ready for the investment but we have yet to get down to the real meat of the process - looking for a property to buy! To make your profit when you buy, you must purchase a property at a price that ensures you make your desired profits based upon your ability to execute your exit strategy. In other words, you need to buy smart. If you vastly overpay for a property, no amount of wishing, hoping, or improvement is going to make your investment worthwhile. You've probably also heard of the term "location is king" in real estate. This chapter will deep dive into how to find a suitable property and how important is the location of a property!

Now that you understand what to look out for in an investment, you need to start actually looking for a property! To get started, you have to first define your search criteria. Defining search criteria is similar to whipping up a great meal. If you want to cook a delicious meal, you will need to purchase the correct ingredients. Sure enough, there can be many variations of ingredients which can whip up an equally delicious meal, but you have to stay focused on making the one meal which appeals to yourself. Buying extra ingredients might result in you turning the dish into something that you don't like and that will be a waste of your money.

The same can be said when you create your list of criteria for real estate investment. You can create different variations of criteria, which work for different people, but there should only be one list, which is most suited for your style of investing. Real estate is an exciting field with a lot of different niches and strategies, so it is easy to get distracted by the next big thing or trend. Having a clearly defined selection criterion can help you stay focused, avoid the "shiny object syndrome" and keep focused on buying the best piece of property. With a clear set of criteria, you can then narrow down your choices in the market and remove many possible deals that serve as distractions. Instead, you can spend all your effort on the kind of properties that you are interested in purchasing. Here are a list of possible criteria which you might want to take in consideration:

- Location
- Property Size in Square Feet
- Property Conditions
- Number of Units

- Cap Rate
- Cash Flow
- Appreciation Potential

You don't have to include everything into your list and nobody is able to tell you which ones should be included in that list. You will have to decide for yourself. The most important thing to consider when choosing your criteria is to think about what kind of investment you want to get into. For example, if you want to micromanage your properties physically, your location is restricted to those that are nearby; if you want a hands off strategy and are inclined towards "buy and hold", then you probably want to place greater emphasis on the appreciation potential and type of your property.

Setting criteria prior to seeking out an investment also makes the searching process much more manageable. With a clearly defined list, you can more effectively communicate your ideas to people who are assisting you in purchasing the property. This can be your real estate agent or investor. You don't want to simply tell people, "I'm looking for a good piece of real estate that can make me money." Instead you want to be specific about the details such as the type, size and location of the property, as well as the budget that you are trying to work within. This makes the job much easier for the other party.

Let's say you already have an ideal list of criteria in mind, there are a few places where you can start looking for your ideal investment. Here is a short list for your reference!

Newspaper. Newspaper may be the oldest form of media communication available and it is quickly fading from use. However, the classified section from your local newspaper still proves to be a good place to look for properties that are on sale.

Networking: Some properties are first put on sale through word of mouth, which is the why it is useful to maintain a little real estate network. This group can consist of people who are property agents, investors, or even family and friends.

Craigslist: Craigslist.org is a free online classifieds website that is currently the #51 most popular website in the world. Millions of people use Craigslist.org to buy, sell, trade, or give away almost anything you can imagine -- including real estate. In fact, I bought my

Outbound Marketing: Outbound marketing involves advertising, direct mail, or a number of other marketing techniques. This is an important technique to bring buyers to sellers.

Location Matters

Location is important when deciding which property to invest in. All too often, an investor stumble on a deal in a city, town, or neighborhood she knows very little about. Here are a few important considerations that will help you choose the most sensible location:

1) *Familiarity* – To be an expert in a specific location, you need to spend a good amount of time in that area. Naturally, our own neighborhoods make a good candidate! Even then, you need to spend the time walking and driving around the streets and doing more research so that you can be confident about your deal. Investing in your neighborhood gives you an advantage over an investor that is out of town because you probably know what the "ins and outs" of the area and understand where a good location to make your investment is.

2) *Proximity* – Being near to your investments is important to effective management. This is especially true of you are new to real estate! Being close to your investment allows you to visit your tenants in short notice and drop by regularly to see how the environment is shaping up. You save on precious time that can be more usefully spent researching on individual properties.

3) *Local Economy* – Ensuring that the local economy is thriving is important because this means that the

purchasing power of the residents is higher. Lower unemployment rates and good paying jobs are two litmus indicator of a thriving, well-off community. This, in turn, leads to low vacancy rates, higher rents and higher property valuations. Always ask your local Realtor what she knows about the employment picture. A good realtor can be a wealth of knowledge about these things since it is integral to her business.

4) *Education* – The availability of good schools are a HUGE driving factors for families to purchase homes in that area. Many parents are willing to pay a premium to gain ease of access to a good education for their kids. If the local government plans on building a school in an area, it could mean that the local housing prices will be on the rise.

The best place to invest is not the same for every person and it is definitely not a simple linear decision. It is individualized based on the areas you are familiar with, where you live, and the properties you already own.

The value of houses is essentially influenced by employment, schools, and gentrification. Study these factors and stick to where they point.

CHAPTER 7.

VALUING PROPERTIES

Before you actually get down to purchasing a property, you have to decide on a fair value, which you are willing to pay. To a new investor, this can be a headache! How do you ensure that you do not undercut your profits? How do you know that you are not losing out on the deal? Let's take a quick look at how property valuations are determined:

1) Sales Comparison Approach (SCA) – SCA is the most common and recognizable way of valuing real estate. In a nutshell, it simply involves comparing the price of your real estate against those that have sold or rented over a certain time frame. The best way to do this is to plot the graph of SCA over a time frame to determine the trend. However, SCA is somewhat generic because every house is intrinsically different from each other. Buyers' and sellers' taste and personal preference also vary greatly. Therefore, the SCA is commonly used as a guideline or reasonable opinion, not an exact evaluator.

2) Capital Asset Pricing Model (CAPM) – CAPM is a more accurate and detailed valuation tool for real estate. The CAPM weaves risk and opportunity cost in to the equation because they are relevant to real estate investing. It essentially looks at the ROI of the prospective investment and compares it to risk-free investments, such as Treasury bonds or REITs. If the estimated ROI of the investment is even lower than the rate of a risk-free investment, then it simply does not make any economic sense to invest in real estate. The CAPM also takes into consideration of the inherent risk involved when you rent out a property. This consideration can depend on the location or age of the real estate. A good example is if the house is located in a place with high crime rate, then is going to affect the cost of maintaining the property.

3) Income Approach – The income approach focuses on the potential rental cash flow a property can generate relative to the initial investment. For example, if the house cost $100,000 to purchase, and you are expected to receive $1,000 in rental cash flow each month, then your annual capitalization rate (Cap rate) is 12% (1000*12/100000). Of course, this is a simplified model that does not take into account of future monetary inflation as well as deflationary risk.

As you can see, your real estate journey can be a very profitable endeavor if you understand the various ways of valuating the properties. Many investors will consider all methods before making an investing decision. Learning these valuation concepts is definitely a step in the right direction!

CHAPTER 8.

MAKING THE OFFER

After you have nailed down the property you want to purchase, it's time to make an official offer. But, where do you start? After all, no one wants to pay more for a house than they should. We all want to get the best deal. Making an offer on a property is like playing a game of chess – every party is waiting on each other to make move, and every move should be calculated. Unlike shopping for ingredients, buying a piece of property has no hard and fast rules, which means there is definitely room for negotiations.

Here is a list of things that should be considered when you are preparing to make an offer:

1) Negotiations: You are always free to negotiate for a price, which you deem to be acceptable. As a general rule of thumb, most investors will start 15-20% below the asking price, assuming that the real estate agent has already added a 10% onto the asking price on what the seller really wants. Don't make a ridiculous offer that severely undercuts the seller, you will only get an angry seller. It is also good to understand the seller's motivation to sell, their preferred settlement date and any other information that may make your offer stronger. For example, the seller may be selling the house due to a termite infestation and you may leverage this scenario to negotiate for a lower price. This is because you need to fork out a sum of money to remove the termites and this cost should be passed on to the seller to a certain extent. The other thing to note is that you should have patience. Don't rush offers unless you have a need to. Showing that you are very urgent usually gives the sense that you are more likely to cave in to price demands, and this can land you in an unfavorable bargaining position.

2) Contingency – Contingencies are conditions that must be satisfied by the seller or the buyer will not be obligated to see through the payment once the offer has been accepted.

Most buyers make an Offer to Purchase (OP) contingent upon their ability to obtain satisfactory mortgage financing. Without this contingency, you could risk losing your earnest money if you cannot get a mortgage loan. Common contingencies include: home inspections, termite inspections, official appraisal etc.

3) Home Inspections – A home inspection is done to determine the condition of structural and mechanical systems of a property. A qualified home inspector should always do this inspection. It is recommended that before you purchase the house, you should include home inspection as a contingency in the Offer of Purchase. Once this is done, you have the option to withdraw the Offer to purchase if the results of the inspection goes south and major problems with the house arises. In fact, it is best to do a house inspection even before you get a bank loan. This way, you can uncover any problems with properties without wasting the time and the finances if it does not work out. A professional home inspection only takes one to three hours (depending on the size of the house), and it gives the buyers some valuable information. To find a professional home inspector, you can reach out to your real estate agent or lender for names with a good reputation.

4) Attorney – After the offer is crafted, it is often a good idea to have an attorney to look over your offer before it gets sent to the seller. If your lawyer discovered any contingencies that are not met, you will have the option of not proceeding with the purchase. Make sure that you protect yourself sufficiently when designing the contingencies, so that you do not regret your decisions later on.

5) Earnest money – The deposit that you are asked to put up front when you submit an offer is called "earnest money". Usually, this amount is paid to the real estate agent first in an escrow account as a show of good faith on your part. Of course, there are cases where the sum is paid to the seller first. This can be resolved between the different parties. If the sale goes through, this earnest money will be deducted from the total amount of money you owe the seller at the end. If the sale falls through, then this earnest money is usually returned.

6) Counteroffer – Once the offer is made, the seller has the choice to accept it as is, reject it or make a counter-proposal. Suppose the seller modifies the terms of the offer, then this is called a counteroffer. The ball will then be in your park to decide if you want to accept it. This is the negotiation process that leads to the final offer that two parties agree. However, most of the time, this negotiation takes place verbally and the offer is only made by the buyer when the price has already been agreed upon.

Chapter 9.

Renting the Space

This is the best part of real estate investing (for some) because this is the phase where you actually start to generate positive cash flow. Renting your house is very profitable and it also makes great economic sense. By renting out your house, you can continue to hold onto your house while the tenant's monthly rent covers the mortgage each month. During this time, the value of your property will hopefully rise to appreciate in value. I've seen too many people buying houses and letting it sit there collecting dust for a few years before selling it. That is a few years' worth of passive income that are being left on the table! Never make the same mistakes.

Of course, putting up your house for rental has its downside as well. There is always a chance that you will receive phone calls at 3am informing you of a leaking pipe as well as cases of tenant consistently delaying payment.

This chapter will provide you with a definitive guide on how to rent your house with the least amount of stress and the best results!

Firstly, you have to decide if you need a property manager to take over the management of the rental property. A property manager will usually charge about 10% of the monthly rent with a 40%-60% of the first month's rent when the tenant moves in. Property manager can take care of advertisements, lease signing, finance tracking or file evictions for you. As a new investor, you might want to start by doing this yourself so that you can adopt a more hands on approach in the learning phase. As your business scales, hiring a property manager will make more sense because of your limited resources.

Next, you have to decide on the rate of your rent. Of course, it is easy to say that you want to collect $10,000 a month but that will be unrealistic. More often than not, the rent is not based on what you as a seller wants, but what the market is willing to pay for. The best way to determine how much your house will rent for is by doing some simple research. A quick search on craigslist will reveal what others in the same region and categories are charging and your rent should be too different from this market rate.

Once you have fixed a rate for your rent, it is time to find suitable tenant candidates. A bad tenant can potentially torment you for years to come while a great tenant can provide years of peace and tranquility. Here are two ways to attract qualified tenants:

1) *Newspaper:* Local newspaper can be a great way to attract tenants. A tip way to reduce the cost of the ad is to learn common abbreviations so that the length of the ad is shortened.

2) *Craigslist.org:* Posting your ad on the web is a great way to attract tenants. The advantage to this is craigslist can possibly have a much wider reach then your local newspaper. You can also put up pictures of your place for free on the site.

If a tenant has reached out to you to enquire on the property, you should always post a few rental criteria to them. For example, let them know how many people can stay in the house at any one time and that they should have a favorable credit history and stable source of income. You can email this list to the prospective tenant and ask them if they meet these qualifications. If they don't – don't rent the house to them. Stand firm to your decision and do not compromise. By allowing tenants to move in who don't meet your criteria, you are only setting yourself up for a long time of misery later on.

If they have passed your initial screening, you may have the candidate tenant fill in an application form to verify that their personal details. You may also use this opportunity to post a series of questions which you think is relevant to you in deciding if your candidate make the cut. Examples of such questions include: Do you have enough cash to pay your first month's rent? How many felonies do you have? Disqualify those that are suitable immediately.

The next step you want to take is to run background and credit checks on the tenant. A background check looks at the tenant's criminal history while a credit check looks at the tenant's ability to pay the bills and fulfil their obligations. You may also wish to set a minimum credit score for you tenants and vary this minimum score based on your location. Another great way you can check on the life of your tenant is by dropping by their current residence unexpectedly to ask for additional signature or pass on a form to fill in. A surprise visit will give insight on how they lead their lives and whether the lifestyle is a good fit for you as a landlord.

If all goes well, you may proceed to let your tenant know that he is successful! Before letting him move in or handing over the keys, be sure to make clear your rules as well as the procedure for paying rent (check or cash).

As a landlord, you have to be responsible for the timely payment of rent, and that your tenants are properly trained to do it in an efficient manner. If things go wrong, seek help! You can always highlight the issue to your attorney, family or real estate agent and they should be able to give you the best possible advice on the next course of action.

CHAPTER 9.

EXIT STRATEGIES

When you purchased the real estate, you should already have an end goal in mind – selling the property for profit or holding the property forever. If you own multiple real estates, chances are, you will want to sell one of them some years down the road. Before you rush into making a sale, it is crucial to realise that deciding on how to sell a real estate property is just as important as deciding which one to buy. In this chapter we will go through 2 of the most common and reliable ways of selling your property.

1) Real Estate Agent – The key here is to find a superstar real estate agent. You want the most suitable agent to sell your property so you can have a peace of mind. After you have found the right person, you need to sign a "listing agreement" with the agent, which states that they have a right to earn the commission if they sell the home. You will then come together to decide on a price to sell it at. Pricing your house is very important and a good agent will be able to compare it with similar houses and accurately determine a good price. Your work at this point of time is not yet finished. Ensure that your house is properly cleaned and furnished so that it has a desirable appearance. The paperwork for the sales transaction is handled by an attorney and if both parties come to an agreement with the price, the deal is closed!

2) Sell through Owner – If you decide that you have the relevant experience or capabilities in selling the house, you can definitely do it yourself! Although a real estate agent will be very convenience because they handle practically everything in the sales transaction, they do take a 6% chunk of commission. If your property is going for a high price, it might make sense for you to try selling it yourself. One of the key disadvantages is that you lose the ability to post your property on the Multiple List Service (MLS), and with it, the ability to reach a wider range of audience because it is only accessible by real estate agents. Of course, if you feel confident of finding a buyer through your private network, selling the property yourself will start to become more appealing.

After going through this 2 ways, you should be fairly familiar with how to get out of a property investment. Of course, there are a few other exit strategies such as Seller Financing and Lease Options. As you move along in your real estate investing career, you will definitely get to learn much more through experience. Remember that as long as you started with the end in mind, you will find that it is much easier to execute your plan when the time is due.

Chapter 10.

Short Case Study

In this chapter, I really want to share with you on how I got started in this and how I made my first successful real estate investment. The reason I want to do this is because I want to show you that this is not a get-rich-quick scheme (as evident from my many failures), however, with the right strategies and hard work, you can definitely paint your own blueprint to a successful passive income business in real estate investing.

I used to be management consultant working for a large firm based out of California. I hated my job because I had to spend time away from my kids and family. I was a good dad, but not a *great* dad. Because of this, I really wanted to spend more time with my family while I can.

So I read up on how I can work from home or create passive sources of income in order to spend time away from the actual work. When I stumbled upon real estate investing, I instantly knew it was right for me! The value of properties around California was on the rise and I was confident that I could do this. So I prepared the money and started to learn everything I can about the business. I connected with real estate agents, attended conference and even paid "gurus" to educate me with their guru knowledge. Not before long, I was already plotting my first investment on a SFH down the street from where I live and the rest is history...

That investment did not go down well because I did not value the property well and ended up overpaying the owners, who also happened to be my friends (couldn't bear to bargain).

Now, here is an investment, which actually turned out well for me.

It was about 7 years ago and I was on the hunt for my next investment. My attention was drawn to a duplex house, which was going for a very reasonable price of $380,000. I immediately contacted the owner to express my interest. The first thing I did was to hire an inspector to inspect the house to make sure that everything is in order and that there is nothing wrong with the system of the house. My criteria is actually fairly straightforward:

1) Town – I want the investment to be local and in close proximity.

2) Neighborhood – I want the distance to grocery shopping and school to be within walking distance of the house

3) Number of Units – The house should be a duplex or triplex

4) Price – Under $500,000

When I saw that the property fulfilled all my criteria, it naturally got me very interested. At that point of time, I could not afford to cough out $420,000 because all my money is tied down in a few investments. So I took a bank loan of about $250,000 to fund this investment. Before actually making the offer, I wanted to make sure that the price that I was paying is fair. I asked my real estate agent to do a quick survey of the prices of the houses in the neighborhood using SCA and it turns out that, the average price of the houses around that area was $550,000! That was a steep discount. Later I discovered that the owner of the house has been relocated out of state and was desperate to sell the property. I didn't do much negotiation and quickly closed the deal because it was indeed a great price. (Today, that house is worth $2,100,000!)

I did a quick refurnishing of the house and posted the pictures and details of the house on craigslist.org and within 2 weeks, I had a whole list of potential candidates. I had to screen them one by one to ensure that I get only the best tenants. Eventually, I decided on a family of three who moved in town because the father just took up a new engineering job in a large software company. I knew that they will be able to afford the bills fairly easily and that they will take good care of the property. For this property, I charged a rate of $3,800 per month and it has been 7 years since I bought it. That's a whopping $300,000 profit just from rent!

This investment truly made me feel that I've chosen the right path and I've never once regretted quitting my day job. Not only am I earning a great income, but I'm also spending a lot more time with my family. I could not have asked for more!

CONCLUSION.

Hopefully through this book, you have gained some precious insight into the world of real estate investment for beginners. We have covered on what exactly is real estate investment and why it is a great investment vehicle. We also walked through on the process of finding a property as well as how to source for financing. You also learnt that finding a good tenant is of paramount importance in determining the level of stress you may encounter throughout the duration of the rental period.

Just by understanding these fundamental concepts, you effectively shortened your learning curve by many years. When I started, I had to learn things the hard way because there was just not that much free information lying around. If you are just getting started right now, the sky is the limit!

Investing in real estate takes a significant amount of effort and you have to be patient to see the results trickling in. Rushing in to make money will only serve to distract you from your eventual goal, which is to make sustainable passive income.

As with everything, it is always very difficult to make the first step. Many people stumbled at the staggering amount they have to cough up just to purchase the first house.

They fear that the money spent will not come back. This fear is unnecessary! In fact, if you fear and do nothing about, it is worse than fear and actually acting on it. The reason is because you are wasting your precious time fearing something, which you are not going to do anyway. Eventually, there has to be a point of time where by you tell yourself to just stop thinking and start doing!

Let that day be today! And good luck.

Can I Ask A Favor? If you enjoyed this book, found it useful or otherwise then I'd really appreciate it if you would post a short review from where you bought it. I do read all the reviews personally so that I can continually write what people are wanting.

If you'd like to leave a review then please visit the link below:

Thanks for your support!

www.ingramcontent.com/pod-product-compliance
Lightning Source LLC
Chambersburg PA
CBHW070920180526
45168CB00005B/2087

Collana: Lavoratori e Imprese

Divieto di concorrenza

per il collaboratore di impresa

- lavoratore subordinato e parasubordinato -

Art. 2105 c.c. primo comma

Con ampia casistica giurisprudenziale

Edizione 2015

Roberto Colantonio

Avvocato